O
THE

by Charlie Josephine

‖SAMUEL FRENCH‖

FOR AMATEUR PRODUCTION ENQUIRIES

UNITED KINGDOM AND WORLD
EXCLUDING NORTH AMERICA
licensing@concordtheatricals.co.uk
020-7054-7298

Each title is subject to availability from Concord Theatricals,
depending upon country of performance.

ONE OF THEM ONES was first performed at Pentabus Theatre, Bromfield, Shropshire, on Thursday 23 March 2023. The cast was as follows:

FRANKIE............................... Em Thane (they/them)
MICHAEL .... Laurie McNamara (he/him)

WRITER................................Charlie Josephine (they/he)
DIRECTOR.................................. Elle While (she/her)
DESIGNER............................. Verity Johnson (they/them)
LIGHTING DESIGNER ....Jen L. Roxburgh (she/her)
SOUND DESIGNER.......................Daniel Balfour (he/him)
MOVEMENT DIRECTOR........................Azara (she/they)
ASSOCIATE DIRECTOR....................Roni Neale (they/them)
/ QUEER CONSULTANT
AUDIO DESCRIPTION CONSULTANT ......Samuel Brewer (he/him)
PRODUCTION MANAGER..................Fiona Hilton (she/her)
STAGE MANAGER.......................Tallulah Harris (she/they)

Produced by Pentabus. *One of Them Ones* was developed with the support of the National Theatre's Generate programme.

Special Thanks to:

Jason Barker, Brillio, Tim Brierley, Lucy Frayne, Vinnie Heaven, Guy Sloan, Rally Training, Gendered Intelligence, Hereford College of Arts, Ludlow Assembly Rooms, Ludlow Homecare.

CAST

EM THANE (THEY/THEM) | FRANKIE
Em trained at East 15 Acting School.

Theatre Credits include: *Beige* (Vault Festival); *What You Will* (The Shakespeare Ensemble); *Same, Same, But Different* (Clapham Fringe Festival).

Film credits include: *Misnomer* (PRISM Short Film Festival).

LAURIE MCNAMARA (HE/HIM) | MICHAEL
Laurie trained at Rose Bruford College. This is Laurie's professional debut.

CREATIVE TEAM

CHARLIE JOSEPHINE (THEY/HE) | WRITER
Charlie Josephine is a writer, director and actor. Charlie is currently under commission with the Royal Shakespeare Company and National Theatre Connections. They are currently writing a play as the Headlong Writer-In-Residence.

Current work includes: *Birds and Bees* (Theatre Centre) and *Flies* (Boundless Theatre).

Previous theatre work includes: *I, Joan* (Shakespeare's Globe); *Moon Licks* (Paines Plough and the Royal Welsh College of Music and Drama); *Pops* (Edinburgh Festival and High Tide Festival); *Blush* (Soho Theatre, Edinburgh Fringe Festival – winning The Stage Edinburgh Award 2016, Camden People's Theatre and on tour); *Bitch Boxer* (Winner of the Soho Theatre Young Writers Award 2012, the Old Vic New Voices Edinburgh Season 2012, the Holden Street Theatre's Award 2013, and the Adelaide Fringe Award 2014).

Charlie won the inaugural BBC Screenplay First Award, and in March 2017 was named on the BBC New Talent Hotlist. They are also currently developing a new feature biopic with Salon Pictures.

Audio work includes: *Massive* (Audible).

ELLE WHILE (SHE/HER) | DIRECTOR
Elle is the Artistic Director of Pentabus Theatre and an Associate Artist of Shakespeare's Globe, she received an MFA in Theatre Directing from Birkbeck College.

Directing includes: *One Of Them Ones*, *Idyll* (Pentabus); *As You Like It* (cbeebies); *Private Peaceful* (Nottingham Playhouse & UK Tour); *The Silence and The Noise*, *Destiny* (Pentabus/Rural Media); *Blue Stockings* (Storyhouse); *The Merry Wives of Windsor*, *As You Like It*, *Hamlet* (Shakespeare's Globe); 2017/2018 Revival director UK, West End International tour of *The Curious Incident of the Dog in the Night-Time* (Gielgud); *What The Moon Saw* (2Faced Dance); *Dance Nation*, *Blindsided*, *RAGE – UK* Premiere (RWCMD); *Wretch* (Shoreditch Church and tour of London homeless shelters); *Glory Dazed* (Soho Theatre, Adelaide Festival and Underbelly, Edinburgh-Winner of Holden St. Theatre award and Critics Choice award); *Country Music* (West Yorkshire Playhouse); *Frisky and Manish: Just Too Much* (Udderbelly, London and Edinburgh); *That Face* (BOVTS); and recording director for the Old Vic's production of *Cause Celebre* on Radio 4.

VERITY JOHNSON (THEY/THEM) | DESIGNER
Verity trained at Wimbledon College of Art. In 2019 Verity was Associate Designer at Nuffield Theatre Southampton.

Theatre credits include: *Educating Yorkshire T'Musical* (BYMT); *Rapture* (Pleasence Theatre); *Andromeda* (Camden People's Theatre); *I Love You, You're Perfect, Now Change* (Chiswick Playhouse); *Easy* (Blue Elephant Theatre); *Fledglings* (Nuffield Theatre); *1984* (Nuffield Theatre); *Maggie May* (Finborough Theatre – Offie Nominated for set design); *Vespertilio* (Vault Festival); *How to Disappear Completely and Never Be Found* (Nuffield Theatre); *The Queen's Nose* (LSMT; Bury The Dead (Finborough Theatre); *Unexpected Joy* (Southwark Playhouse); *Half Me Half You* (Wild Project, NYC); *Mermaids* (King's Head Theatre); *Nine Foot Nine* (Bunker Theatre); *Hilda and Virginia* (Jermyn Street Theatre); *Testament* (Vault Festival); *The House of Usher* (The Hope Theatre); *The Dumb Waiter* (Maltings Arts Theatre).

As an assistant: *Hamlet*, *As You Like It* (Shakespeare's Globe); *The Audience* (Nuffield Theatre); *Rotterdam* (The Arts Theatre); *German Skerries* (Orange Tree Theatre); *Microcosm* (Soho Theatre).

As studio assistant to: Tim Hatley, Nicky Shaw, Netia Jones, Sara Perks, and Rosie Elnile.

JEN L. ROXBURGH (SHE/HER) | LIGHTING DESIGNER

Jen was awarded the BBC Performing Arts 'Ones to Watch' fellowship in Lighting Design with English Touring Theatre. Theatre work includes: *Destiny* (National Tour); *Old Market (REMIXED)* (Wardrobe Theatre); *Cockroach* (Jacksons Lane) and, *The Stranger on the Bridge* (Postcard Productions at Tobacco Factory Theatre). *Blame Game* (Kundle Kru on a European Tour) and *Look, No Hands* (Summerhall, Edinburgh).

DAN BALFOUR (HE/HIM) | SOUND DESIGN AND COMPOSITION

Dan has received 4 OFFIE 'Best Sound Design' nominations for his work on *Operation Mincemeat* (New Diorama); *The Tempest* (Pleasance); *Great Apes* (Arcola); *Blood Wedding* (Omnibus).

Theatre credits include: *Wuthering Heights* (Inspector Sands); *How To Break Out Of A Detention Centre* (Riverside Studios); *One That Wants To Cross* (Finborough); *Assembly* (Wayward Productions); *Wipe These Tears* (Bézna Theatre); *Les Dawson: Flying High* (So Television, Ed Fringe and National Tour); *I AM KEVIN* (WildWorks); *The Dance of Death* (Theatre Royal Bath and UK Tour); *The Misfortune of The English* (Orange Tree Theatre); *LAVA* (UK Tour); *Tempest* (Pleasance Theatre); *Private Peaceful* (Nottingham Playhouse & UK Tour); *The Hatchling* (Trigger Productions); *Idyll* (Pentabus); *Two Character Play* (Hampstead Theatre); *Can I Live* (Complicité); *Voices Of The Earth* (Complicité); *Cinderella, Robin Hood, Beauty And The Beast* (Oxford Playhouse); *Fahrenheit 451* (RCSSD); *Sugar Syndrome* (Orange Tree); *Pavilion* (Theatre Clwyd); *HOME* (Young Vic); *Counting Sheep* (Belarus Free Theatre); *hang* (Sheffield Crucible); *Wilderness* (Hampstead Theatre); *Operation Mincemeat* (New Diorama Theatre, Southwark Playhouse); *Effigies Of Wickedness* (Gate Theatre); *Great Apes* (Arcola Theatre); *VINOVAT, -Ä* (Teatru Replica, Bucharest).

AZARA (SHE/THEY) | MOVEMENT DIRECTOR

Azara is a multi-disciplinary artist working with live art and film, poetry, breakdancing and theatre. Azara has worked with artists including: playwright Roy Williams; Company 3; David Hoyle; Ursula Martinez; Duckie; Ella Mesma Company and Some Voices. Azara has also performed as a dancer at Sadler's Wells Theatre and The London Olympic Opening Ceremony 2012.

Azara's first live solo performance *I Am A Woman* was created in Jamaica, a video adaptation of the piece screened at festivals across London, Berlin and New York including the BFI Flare Film Festival. Azara went on to create another solo performance called *Just Another Day and Night* (UK tour).

Other theatre credits include: *Run It Back* (Talawa Theatre Company); *Finding Grace* (Thick & Tight Dance); *I, Joan* (Shakespeare's Globe) and *The Dog Show* (The Pleasance).

RONI NEALE (THEY/THEM) | ASSOCIATE DIRECTOR / QUEER CONSULTANT

Roni is a transgender theatremaker from Dorset. Their debut play, *Indecent Acts*, was commissioned by Shire Hall as part of a British Museum touring exhibition, and will be published in an anthology of trans work. Neale is currently developing work with the National Youth Theatre on transgender youth and anti-transgender conspiracy theorists. Their show Misstrial, directed by Jamie Fletcher (Hedwig and the Angry Inch) was showcased at the QueerCoreHomotopia Festival 2021, supported by Homotopia and the Liverpool Everyman & Playhouse.

SAMUEL BREWER (HE/HIM) | AUDIO DESCRIPTION CONSULTANT

Samuel is an access consultant, facilitator, actor & theatre maker who trained at The Royal Central School of Speech and Drama. Samuel co-founded the award winning disability led theatre company FlawBored who are Theatre Deli resident artists and Pleasance Associate Artists. With FlawBored Samuel developed and devised their debut show *It's a motherf***king pleasure*. Samuel has worked as a theatre maker and actor for numerous companies such as Asylum Arts, Complicité, The Watermill Theatre, Told by an idiot amongst others.

PENTABUS

'Pentabus is probably one of the most important theatre companies in the country, where it has led, other new writing theatres – such as the Royal Court – have followed' – The Telegraph

Pentabus is the nation's rural theatre company. We are the only professional theatre company in the UK whose vision is singularly rural. We tour new plays about the contemporary rural world to new audiences in village halls, fields, festivals and theatres, telling stories with local relevance, plus national and international impact.

We believe that every person living in an isolated rural community has a right to exceptional theatre. We are based in a Victorian school in rural Shropshire, and to date all of our work has been made here. It then tours village halls and theatres locally and nationally. Over four and a half decades we've produced more than 300 new plays, reached over half a million audience members, won a prestigious South Bank Show award, a Fringe First and were the first to live stream from a village hall. We have hosted a writer in residence since 2014 and they have gone on to be commissioned by the Birmingham Rep, the Bush, HighTide, Nottingham Playhouse, the National Theatre, Royal Court and Royal Welsh College.

We are a champion for rural young people aged 16 to 30 and Pentabus Young Company is our programme offering workshops, masterclasses, work experience and mentorships, as well as the opportunity to join our Young Writers' Group, which has been running for ten years. Previous participants of the Young Writers' Group have had their work presented at Ludlow Fringe, Latitude Festival and Hereford Courtyard. It is a springboard into further study and the arts industry.

You can find out more about us at:

pentabus.co.uk

Twitter: @pentabustheatre
Facebook: @pentabustheatre
Instagram: @Pentabustheatrecompany

Pentabus Theatre Company, Bromfield, Ludlow, Shropshire, SY8 2JU

CHARACTERS

FRANKIE – They/He. 18 years old. AFAB, nonbinary, trans masc. Working class, Herefordian. Strong and sweet, with wide eyed wonder.

MICHAEL – He/Him. 23 years old. Cis straight man. Frankie's big brother. Working class. Cheeky and charming, with a big heart.

AUTHOR'S NOTES

When Pentabus Theatre approached me to write a play for them I knew instantly that I wanted to write a queer love story. Because the heteroghetto is wild right now, especially in the UK, it's a very challenging time to be trans and queer. But the love is always louder than the fear, and I believe in the power of good theatre. We are changed by hearing people's stories. Culture changes culture. So I'm honoured to have the opportunity to tour this queer and trans story to rural venues. It's such a terrible myth that queerness is just found in cities! It's been a privilege to meet some of the incredible LGBTQ+ people in and around Ludlow whilst developing this script. I'm grateful for their courage and their honesty. I was surprised to find myself writing about family love rather than romantic love, but these two brothers fell out of my pen. I wanted to write something working class and down to earth. I wanted to write something funny and tender and sticky-messy in its honesty. I'm really proud of the piece we have made and I'm excited to share it with new audiences.

Script Note

Stage directions are in italics and brackets.

A / indicates a fast run onto the next line, almost an interruption.

A /... indicates where a word can't be found and the actor does something physical to express themself. It could be a small pedestrian gesture or a big abstract movement.

A . indicates where a character should have a line, but is choosing not to speak.

THANK YOUS

Thank you to Elle for your humour and open heart. Thank you to Sean Holmes for the link up. Thank you as always to Jonathan at the agency for your care. Thank you to Vinnie Heaven for your brilliant work during an R&D at the National Theatre Studios. Thank you to Laurie and Em for your brilliant performances. Thank you Rye Frankie Larsen for your beautiful artwork. Thank you to all the gorgeous rural LGBTQ+ people that we met to develop the play.

for Pentabus Theatre, spring 2023

(They enter the space and look at us. Honest in their nervousness, but ready to be seen. They speak to us where possible, inviting us into the story.)

MICHAEL. *(To him.)* You walk in. And/

FRANKIE. *(To him.)* we look at each other, and/

BOTH. *(To him.)* we know.

MICHAEL. *(To us.)* We both know/

FRANKIE. *(To us.)* that *this* is a Big moment.

MICHAEL. *(To us.)* Huge!

FRANKIE. *(To us.)* This feels, huge! And I feel/

MICHAEL. *(To him.)* awake?

FRANKIE. *(To him.)* Yeah!

MICHAEL. *(To us.)* Suddenly, really awake, to everything?

FRANKIE. *(To him.)* Yeah, like, aware?

MICHAEL. *(To him.)* Yeah! Aware!

FRANKIE. *(To us.)* Like all the colours are brighter and, the lines and shapes and/

MICHAEL. *(To us.)* everything's clearer, somehow?

FRANKIE. Yeah!

MICHAEL. We're there, in front of each other, standing/

FRANKIE. toe to toe/

MICHAEL. yeah/

FRANKIE. nose to nose/

MICHAEL. yeah/

FRANKIE. soul to soul!

MICHAEL. *(Joking.)* I dunno about that.

FRANKIE. And I look/

MICHAEL. into your eyes. And you look/

FRANKIE. into mine.

MICHAEL. And I see/

FRANKIE. you seeing/

BOTH. me.

MICHAEL. And something inside of me is telling me to pay attention, to watch this moment we're in because we know, somehow, *this* moment is significant. *This* moment is big!

FRANKIE. Huge!

MICHAEL. Yeah, like you know you're gonna wanna tell people later about this moment. So you're paying attention, cus you know/

FRANKIE. somehow you *know,* that *this* right here/

MICHAEL. right now/

FRANKIE. could be the start/

MICHAEL. or the end/

FRANKIE. of/

MICHAEL. something, of/

FRANKIE. everything.

> *(Shift in space. Their bodies start moving. Pulsing and bouncing. Something is building inside them. They speak to us.)*

MICHAEL. And like, to be fair right, I'm like, both relieved/

FRANKIE. and scared/

MICHAEL. and scared, that we're about to do this. About to have this conversation. Because we know that some things are gonna be said/

FRANKIE. that *need* to be said/

MICHAEL. but will be hard to say/

FRANKIE. and even harder to hear.

MICHAEL. Yeah.

FRANKIE. And, to be honest, I don't actually even know where to start?

MICHAEL. I dunno where to start!

FRANKIE. So/

MICHAEL. we/

BOTH. both/

MICHAEL. start/

FRANKIE. speaking/

BOTH. at the same time.

FRANKIE. And it's chaos! All adrenaline and/

MICHAEL. noise noise noise!

FRANKIE. I can't hear you!

MICHAEL. I don't even know what *I'm* saying!

FRANKIE. But I *do* know that this/

MICHAEL. is *not* a good start! You're like/

FRANKIE. *(To him.)* I need to talk to you. *(To us.)* But you're like/

MICHAEL. *(To him.)* no!

FRANKIE. *(To us.)* Just, no?

MICHAEL. *(To us.)* No. *(To him.)* I don't wanna hear it! I don't give a fuck!

FRANKIE. *(To us.)* And that?! That's when it all kicks off!

> *(Burst of movement. Frenetic and fast. Energy is bursting up and out of their bodies, electric and fizzy and hot. It zaps up their spine and out their limbs. A rare glimpse into the inner animal of all humans. It makes us gasp in it's honesty. Then suddenly it's gone and they're stood still, staring at each other, breathless.)*

MICHAEL. No! I don't wanna hear it! I don't give a fuck!

FRANKIE. Oh nice one! Meant to be my brother/

MICHAEL. and *what are you?!*

FRANKIE. What?!

MICHAEL. What is this? What is *happening* to you?! I don't even /... I don't get it, I don't even *want* to get it!

FRANKIE. Well that's the problem isn't it?!

MICHAEL. No, the problem is *you* causing dramas the day before my wedding! I'm getting *married!* Tomorrow!

FRANKIE. I know!

MICHAEL. So what the hell Frankie?! Of all the times/

FRANKIE. I've *tried* to tell you! I've tried to explain it, over and over, for *months* now/

MICHAEL. I just want a peaceful life! You know? Lovely! Calm, quiet little life. No drama, no stress/

FRANKIE. well we all want that don't we?! But it's a little more complicated for some of us. Look, I'm not finding any of this easy, OK?! This whole thing? It's /... I dunno, it's hard! But I need to stand up for myself, I need to start doing the things that I/

MICHAEL. oh my God?! Can you for once not make it *all* about you?!

FRANKIE. I'm not/

MICHAEL. can you *please*, just turn up and sit there or stand there or whatever, but just *not* make it *all* about you?! Just once?! On my *wedding* day? Can you do that?!

FRANKIE. I'll be there. But I won't wear it. I can't!

MICHAEL. Look, I don't give a shit what you're wearing/

FRANKIE. great/

MICHAEL. but Tasha does. And I'm gonna give her the Dream Wedding that she's always wanted!

FRANKIE. Course you are.

MICHAEL. Oh, what the does that mean?

FRANKIE. Nothin'! I just/

MICHAEL. you've *never* given her a chance.

FRANKIE. I have!

MICHAEL. You have *no idea* how much this means to her. Seriously! Ever since she was little she's been wanting this/

FRANKIE. but *why* it matter if I/

MICHAEL. she picked out all the dresses! The suits, the flowers thc, the fucking *everything!* And if she wants you all looking the same, then all you girls have gotta be/

FRANKIE. I'm not a girl.

MICHAEL. Fucksake!

FRANKIE. I've *tried* to tell you!

MICHAEL. I can't handle this/

FRANKIE. but you won't listen/

MICHAEL. just wear the dress!

FRANKIE. Please, just *listen!*

MICHAEL. No *you* just listen!

FRANKIE. I can *explain,* if you/

MICHAEL. I don't wanna fucking know Frankie! I don't wanna hear it! I don't give a fuck! I honestly do not give a fuck about whatever the fuck it is you're doing! All this?! Attention seeking drama bullshit *again?!* Honestly? I'm done!

FRANKIE. What?!

MICHAEL. You're *fucking* selfish! You're always so fucking selfish making *everything* about you *all* the time?! It's unbelievable! Can't even let me have just *one* day? Have to ruin everything?

FRANKIE. I don't/

MICHAEL. you *ruin, everything!*

> *(They stare at each other. Both hurting.* **MICHAEL** *turns away. He picks up his paint roller and speak to the floor.)*

I need to finish this. Before tonight. So can you just go yeah?

> *(**MICHAEL** starts painting the wall. **FRANKIE** hesitates, before turning to leave. **FRANKIE** speaks to us.)*

FRANKIE. So, that's our introduction. That's how this all started. I mean, obviously this had been building for years. All families have their stuff, right? But that's how *this* story starts, with *that* moment, where everything in him exploded, and all this ugly shit came spilling out, and he was finally honest, about how he sees me. And

like, I'd never seen him be this ugly, he's *never* been so
/... And once he'd said it, you could tell, once the words
started tripping off his tongue and flying out his mouth
there was this flash of fear on his face, his eyes told me
he regretted it but too late! Cus once you spill out like
that? Nah, you can't take it back. And once I'd heard
it, I couldn't ever unhear it. Something was changed,
in that moment, something was like, forever different.
And, yeah, I could have left. I probably should have.

MICHAEL. *(Over his shoulder.)* I wanted you to.

FRANKIE. Did you?

MICHAEL. Yeah!

FRANKIE. Did you really though?

MICHAEL. Yes!

FRANKIE. .

MICHAEL. Probably not.

FRANKIE. *(To us.)* So yeah, I could have left. I probably/

MICHAEL. why didn't you? I mean, I was 'orrible. Really,
fucking, /...

FRANKIE. Mum.

MICHAEL. What?

FRANKIE. Mum said she'd kill me if I didn't go sort it out
right now, and like, no offence but, she scares me more
than you do.

MICHAEL. Fair enough!

FRANKIE. Yeah, it's all thanks to mum really. Or we'd still
hate each other.

MICHAEL. I never hated you, I just/

FRANKIE. I know. *(To us.)* So anyway, I could have left. Or
he could have apologised.

MICHAEL. *You* could have!

FRANKIE. He could have taken responsibility for his narrow minded view of the/

MICHAEL. oh shuttup!

FRANKIE. *You* shut up!

MICHAEL. You're a dickead!

FRANKIE. *You* are!

MICHAEL. *(To us.)* Anyway! Why don't we just move on to the next bit?

FRANKIE. *(To him.)* Fine! *(To us.)* Here's what happened next.

> (**MICHAEL** *paints the wall.* **FRANKIE** *finds some overalls in one of the bags and start pulling them on.)*

MICHAEL. No! No Frankie/

FRANKIE. lemme help you/

MICHAEL. no! Stop messin' about/

FRANKIE. it'll be way quicker if I/

MICHAEL. no! I told you to go! So just go yeah/

FRANKIE. yeah well I ain't going nowhere! Alright? Cus I really fucking need you to get this! I really fucking *need* you, to *see* me! And so I ain't going 'til we talk about it/

MICHAEL. well then you'll be here forever/

FRANKIE. fine/

MICHAEL. cus I ain't getting into all that, and there's nothin' to talk about anyway!

FRANKIE. Fine!

MICHAEL. Fine!

(**FRANKIE** *zips up the overalls, defiant.*
MICHAEL *turns his back on* **FRANKIE** *and
furiously paints the wall.* **FRANKIE** *takes a
deep breath then picks up a roller and paints
the wall next to* **MICHAEL**. *They paint in
silence. Both doing their best i-am-angry-
painting. After a while a song comes on the
radio that they both really like. They try not
to, but they just can't help themselves, and
they shyly sing along a little to it. The song
softens them, despite their best efforts to stay
angry. By the second chorus they're fully
enjoying a duet, laughing at each other.*)

FRANKIE. He's always had the moves!

MICHAEL. You know it!

FRANKIE. So macho it's almost camp!

MICHAEL. You what?

FRANKIE. You know, like extreme masculinity? Like those
guys you see at the gym sweating and grunting and /...
It's like, actually quite camp, in its masculine-ness?

MICHAEL. If you say so.

(**MICHAEL** *turns away from* **FRANKIE**, *who
feels rejected but knows not to push it. They
paint together.* **FRANKIE** *tries a new tactic.*)

FRANKIE. This place is *well* fancy!

MICHAEL. .

FRANKIE. Wouldn't mind a house like this one day eh?

MICHAEL. .

FRANKIE. They a big client then yeah?

MICHAEL. Obviously!

FRANKIE. Obviously.

MICHAEL. Look I haven't got time/

FRANKIE. I'm not/

MICHAEL. for you to be messing about/

FRANKIE. No I'm *not*/

MICHAEL. I *have* to get this done! Today! We're already a week late cus Pete's been fuckin' about, and I've been trying to sort the wedding/

FRANKIE. where is Pete?

MICHAEL. He's gone. Dave pulled him of the job/

FRANKIE. What? Why?!

MICHAEL. Dunno, they had a barny, Dave put his foot down, Pete's gone.

FRANKIE. Fuck!

MICHAEL. Yeah. So now I'm stuck trying to get it done/

FRANKIE. yeah but, can't it wait 'til next week or/

MICHAEL. no.

FRANKIE. But like, your wedding?

MICHAEL. I know!

FRANKIE. Ain't that like, special circumstances?

MICHAEL. Dave don't think so. He's raving. Threatening to sack me n all if I don't get it done.

FRANKIE. What? No, that's not on/

MICHAEL. I know/

FRANKIE. you don't have to put up with/

MICHAEL. don't tell me what to do when you don't know! You're a kid! You don't know/

FRANKIE. nah but honestly he can't do that/

MICHAEL. If I don't finish it today, then I don't get paid. Don't have a job no more. Simple as that. And then there'll be no wedding tomorrow, got bills coming out me arse, be no wedding *ever*, cus Tash will kill me! She'd be heart-broke! So if you're helping then help, and if you ain't then/

FRANKIE. I am, I am!

MICHAEL. Great.

FRANKIE. .

MICHAEL. .

>   (**FRANKIE** *tries a new tactic.*)

FRANKIE. This is harder than I thought.

MICHAEL. .

FRANKIE. You're pretty good at it.

MICHAEL. .

FRANKIE. Got all the tips and tricks from college I guess?

MICHAEL. Barely! College is shit.

FRANKIE. Oh. So I guess Dave's been training you well/

MICHAEL.   he wishes! Ain't taught me nothin'! Apprenticeship my arse. I'm self-taught! YouTube videos and that, learning on the job. *(Turns on* **FRANKIE**, *suddenly stern.)* It's hard graft this!

FRANKIE. Yeah.

MICHAEL. No messing about!

FRANKIE. Yeah, can see that yeah.

>   (**MICHAEL** *turns back to his painting.*
>   **FRANKIE** *shares a giggle with us, then hides
>   it quickly.)*

Oh my God, d'you remember when Pete nearly got us killed by them White-Cross lads?!

MICHAEL. What an idiot!

FRANKIE. He was all like, *"I'm not being funny lads but this is our pitch. We play here every week. So you're/"*

BOTH. *"just gonna have to piss off!"*

MICHAEL. *"Cus we aint got time to be pissing about!"*

FRANKIE. No, fannying about he said!

MICHAEL. Haha yeah!

FRANKIE. *"We ain't got time to be Fannying about with a bunch of Silly Little Boys who think they're hard!"*

MICHAEL. Oooh! When he said that I knew it was trouble!

FRANKIE. I know! It were like a western!

MICHAEL. Yeah this like, moment of silence, this like *pause!* Where no one done nothin', just staring at each other?!

FRANKIE. Yeah I'm looking at them/

MICHAEL. and they're looking at me/

FRANKIE. and we're all tryna look braver than we really are!

MICHAEL. Yeah! Everyone's holding their breath!

FRANKIE. Like fuck!

MICHAEL. Fuck!

FRANKIE. Can't *believe* Pete just said that!

MICHAEL. Fuck!

FRANKIE. Fuck!

MICHAEL. What's gonna happen next?

FRANKIE. This moment of dramatic tension/

MICHAEL. building and building and building/

FRANKIE. like we're in a movie/

MICHAEL. yeah like who's gonna shoot first?

    (They are suddenly cowboys at a shoot out.)

FRANKIE. Then suddenly/

MICHAEL. suddenly/

FRANKIE. one of the White Cross lads hocks up this greenie!

MICHAEL. Massive gross greenie! From the back of his nose/

FRANKIE. ugh! Don't!

MICHAEL. Down his throat!

FRANKIE. Don't!

MICHAEL. Into his mouth. And he/

BOTH. gobs it/

MICHAEL. onto the floor/

FRANKIE. splat!

MICHAEL. Right next to Pete's trainers!

FRANKIE. Shit!

MICHAEL. This greenie sat shining on the concrete.

FRANKIE. Ugh!

MICHAEL. Then everyone looks at the lad who gobbed it.

FRANKIE. Then everyone looks at Pete.

MICHAEL. Then everyone and everything explodes!

    (They burst into a stylised gunfight, bursting across the space shooting at imaginary bad guys. Then they throw away their guns and

shift into a Kung-Fu style fight sequence that gets more and more elaborate. Suddenly **FRANKIE** *points outwards.)*

FRANKIE. Police!

BOTH. Shit!

(They both start running on the spot.)

MICHAEL. And everyone legs it!

FRANKIE. Bursting this way and that!

MICHAEL. Across the field/

FRANKIE. across the carpark/

MICHAEL. up over the fence/

FRANKIE. or under it/

MICHAEL. either way/

BOTH. just run!

MICHAEL. Heart thumping!

FRANKIE. Sweat flying!

MICHAEL. Trainers pounding on concrete!

FRANKIE. Down the back streets/

MICHAEL. and up the alleyways/

FRANKIE. through the hole in the fence/

MICHAEL. that gives us a sneaky shortcut/

FRANKIE. that only *we* know about/

MICHAEL. cus *we* know this town/

FRANKIE. like the/

BOTH. back of our hand!

MICHAEL. Faster faster!

FRANKIE. Up by the garages/

MICHAEL. faster faster!

FRANKIE. Down the back of the shops/

MICHAEL. faster faster! Shit! Where's Frankie?! Is Frankie OK? *Where's Frankie?!* Has anyone/

FRANKIE. burst out a side street, can't catch me, lightning fast feet, don't even take a beat, keep running and running and tearing up concrete!

MICHAEL. *Frankie!*

FRANKIE. See you up ahead, see you with the lads, see you seeing me, relieved/

MICHAEL. *oh! You're there!*

FRANKIE. Fly across the road/

MICHAEL. *LOOK OUT!*

FRANKIE. And/

BOTH. *OH MY GOD!*

MICHAEL. Eyes wide/

FRANKIE. and breath caught/

MICHAEL. trainers skidding/

FRANKIE. on asphalt/

MICHAEL. screech/

FRANKIE. to a stop/

MICHAEL. nose/

FRANKIE. to nose/

MICHAEL. with a milk float!

FRANKIE. Hahaha imagine getting knocked down by a milk float! So cringe! Like a sports car or range rover fine, but a milk float?!

MICHAEL. Lucky it was a milk float they only go about two miles an hour!

FRANKIE. Yeah maybe. Still a bit cringe though!

MICHAEL. Yeah!

FRANKIE. And when we all saw each other later/

MICHAEL. down the pub, pints and crisps and/

FRANKIE. long winded tales of our individual adventures/

MICHAEL. *"I took on three of 'em!"*

FRANKIE. *"Three? I took on seven!"*

MICHAEL. *"Aye and I got a rocket ship to the moon!"* Silly sod!

FRANKIE. Falling about laughing at each other/

MICHAEL. and making Pete get the round in/

FRANKIE. cus he started it!

BOTH. *"I never!"* … You bloody did!

MICHAEL. Ah yeah! That was a good day!

FRANKIE. It was 'mazin'! I was proper one of the lads.

MICHAEL. .

FRANKIE. Like yeah, it was a proper laugh, weren't it?

> (**MICHAEL** *turns back to his painting.* **FRANKIE** *doesn't seem to notice or mind* **MICHAEL**'s *rejection.* **FRANKIE** *wanders about, having a stretch. He feels the overalls he's wearing.)*

I like these.

> (**MICHAEL** *glances at* **FRANKIE**, *but doesn't give him attention.)*

It's cool you get to wear this everyday like.

(**FRANKIE** *starts strutting up and down, playing the model.*)

Yeah! Ooh yeah! Feels good!

MICHAEL. You gonna do this work or what?

(**FRANKIE** *poses and plays.* **MICHAEL** *frowns, very serious.*)

Stop messing about! This is my job!

FRANKIE. I know!

MICHAEL. You can't just come in here and pick up my stuff, start wearing my clothes/

FRANKIE. *"get out of my room Frankie!"*

MICHAEL. *(Stunned.)* What?!

FRANKIE. *"Frankie! Get out of my room!" (To us.)* He was always so territorial about his space. Never let me play with his toys, I wasn't even allowed to touch them.

MICHAEL. cus you broke everything!

FRANKIE. Your room was so cool! All the toys and the colours and the everything! I'd sneak in there just to look around, and touch everything/

MICHAEL. I knew it! I knew it was you doing that/

FRANKIE. like maybe I could suck up some of the coolness through my fingertips?

MICHAEL. Don't touch my stuff!

FRANKIE. Maybe it'd help me be more like you? I mean, you were my hero.

MICHAEL. .

FRANKIE. Still are, I guess. I remember once, you must have been out playing? I dunno. But I've snuck in your room and /... I can't explain it, it's like, I'm just *compelled* to? I'm compelled, to put on your school clothes. Mum's letting me wear what I want at home, but I've got to wear girls' uniform at school. And I *hate* it. And I've tried, *everything*, but, there's *nothing* I can do, because adults are bigger than kids and they don't listen, they don't realise it really does hurt when we say something's hurting. Anyway, you're out or whatever, I'm alone and I pull on your clothes. Can still remember the fabric. Polyester, grey, school trousers. The zip and the button under my thumbs. Crinkled school shirt, you'd chucked on the floor, rejected, in favour of vest and football shorts. My hands on the fabric, still warm from your skin all day at school, and I get a glimpse into maybe what it's like to be you. And I wonder if you know how lucky you are? Like, have you even got a clue? Cus *these* clothes? They felt, *magic* to me, they felt/

> (*Movement sneaks out of* **FRANKIE***'s body during the above monologue and by the end they are fully swept up in the memory. Dance bursts out of him. Gender euphoria. Spiritual recharge. Cheeky and joyful, enjoying his masculinity, playing and taking up space. It builds and builds. Then suddenly* **MICHAEL** *physically stops* **FRANKIE***, embarrassed by something.*)

You're embarrassed.

MICHAEL. No.

FRANKIE. You are. Can feel it, in my belly. Can feel your embarrassment in my belly/

MICHAEL. no, I said no!

> (**FRANKIE** *sits down on a paint pot, sulking.* **MICHAEL** *looks at them, then looks at us.*)

(To us.) I'm not the Bad Guy. Just so you know. I know like in every story there's meant to be a Bad Guy and a Good/

FRANKIE. what are you doing?

MICHAEL. I don't want them just thinking I'm a dick!

FRANKIE. They won't.

MICHAEL. Well you keep doing bits that make me look bad.

FRANKIE. I keep doing bits that are *truthful!* And yeah OK some of them don't make you look great but that's cus you didn't act great. I'm not gonna rewrite history so you look better!

MICHAEL. Why not?

FRANKIE. Michael/

MICHAEL. you said we'd be doing this together!

FRANKIE. We are!

MICHAEL. Then how comes you're doing loads of talkin', to them, alone?

FRANKIE. A monologue.

MICHAEL. What?

FRANKIE. It's called a, it doesn't matter/

MICHAEL. you keep talking to them, telling them stuff?

FRANKIE. You can too. If you want.

MICHAEL. Fine, I will.

> (**MICHAEL** *turns to us, but hesitates. He shoo's* **FRANKIE** *away.)*

Go away then!

FRANKIE. Oh right!

(**FRANKIE** *buries their head in the paint colour chart books.* **MICHAEL** *turns to us.*)

MICHAEL. *(To us.)* I erm, hello. OK. Well, I don't, I mean, obviously I don't usually do stuff like this I /... This was Frankie's idea, and, I got talked into it, as per usual. Frankie said we should do this, tell our story, cus yeah, it's a mad one, and maybe someone might like it, and find it useful or whatever? So, that's why we're here. And yeah, I guess this is my bit. Cus yeah, I just wanna say that, I know I look like a bit of a dick at the start, of the story like, because, well yeah, I was a bit of a dick. Not cus I *am* a dick, but just cus like I dunno it's mad?! Like, bloody 'ell! It's *a lot* to get your head round, you know?! Cus like, yeah, like that's my little sister.

FRANKIE. *(Without looking up.)* Brother.

(**MICHAEL** *looks at* **FRANKIE**, *then speaks to us. Trying to find the words.*)

MICHAEL. When mum was pregnant, with you, I used to lay my head on her tummy. And you'd always kick for me. You never would kick for anyone else, but when I put my head there you'd start kicking away, always tryna boot me in the ear from like day one! *Will the baby be a boy, or a girl?* I'd ask mum over and over. *Will I have a little brother, or a little sister*? It doesn't matter, she said, we'll love them either way, and you'll be their big brother, you'll be there to take care of them. Which felt like, wow! /... And when the day came, I wore my best shirt to the hospital. Wanted to look smart, when I met you. And, oh! /... This *huge* feeling in my chest! Made it go all like, bigger inside? Like, huge?! /... I kissed your head, ever so gentle. And you wrapped your tiny hand around my finger, look! I whispered in your ear, I'm your big brother, you're my little sister.

(**MICHAEL** *looks at* **FRANKIE**, *then begins painting again.* **FRANKIE** *is still flicking through the colour charts.*)

FRANKIE. I love the names of colours!

MICHAEL. .

FRANKIE. Cotton Breeze. Purple Pout. Elephant's Breath!

MICHAEL. You doing any work or what?

FRANKIE. Apricot Crush. Copper Blush. Ooh Soft Peach, that's nice, look!

MICHAEL. *(Sarcastic.)* Lovely!

FRANKIE. Nordic Sky... Sea Blue, Sapphire Salute, ooh, Quintessential Blue.

MICHAEL. You what?

FRANKIE. Quintessential. Means like, perfect. Like the perfect something, I think. Hang on. Siri what does quintessential mean?

(Siri answers.)

Yes! Told you.

MICHAEL. Clever clogs.

FRANKIE. That's a good one, Clever Clogs. That'd be like, a grey I guess? Or a brown?

MICHAEL. Don't ask me, I just put it on the walls.

FRANKIE. Moon Cloud! Misty Mountain. Muddy Puddle.

MICHAEL. Nah!

FRANKIE. What?

MICHAEL. No one wants that!

FRANKIE. They do, I bet they do, it's a nice colour, look.

MICHAEL. Yeah but, like *"oooh what colours your walls mate?"* Muddy Puddle. *"Lovely!"* Nah, don't think so! No one's gonna be like that!

FRANKIE. I am.

MICHAEL. Well you're a nutter.

FRANKIE. Vanilla Sundae, nice... Butter Biscuit! Cookie Dough. Mmmm Cranberry Crunch!

MICHAEL. It's not a dinner menu!

FRANKIE. Dusted Cappuccino! Berry Smoothie!

MICHAEL. You can't eat it!

FRANKIE. Shame, it's making me hungry! ... Who gets to name the colours? That's a job ain't it. Whoever's got that job is dead jammy. I would love that. I'd be well good at that!

MICHAEL. Would ya.

FRANKIE. Yeah! Like, Caramel Dream. Or, or Spiced, Walnut. Or Dusty Sunrise.

MICHAEL. Dusty Sunrise?

FRANKIE. Alright maybe not.

MICHAEL. Don't give up the day job mate! Oh yeah, I forgot, you ain't got a job. Still scrounging off mum!

FRANKIE. You live there too!

MICHAEL. That's temporary!

FRANKIE. Kipping on the sofa! Can't even watch the telly!

MICHAEL. You *love* having me home.

FRANKIE. Nah! It's well cramped!

MICHAEL. Well I'll be gone soon

FRANKIE. Good!

MICHAEL. Tasha and me will have our own place. Soon as I can afford a deposit.

FRANKIE. Why don't you just take the money that her dad said/

MICHAEL. no! No way. I ain't taking a penny from him!

FRANKIE. Alright!

MICHAEL. And anyway I pay mum rent, what d'you contribute eh?

FRANKIE. I'm a student!

MICHAEL. Student my arse! Getting stoned all day long/

FRANKIE. I don't/

MICHAEL. and chatting about politics or whatever/

FRANKIE. we don't/

MICHAEL. while the rest of us are grafting!

FRANKIE. I work really hard actually!

MICHAEL. Yeah sure sure.

> (**FRANKIE** *rolls their eyes and turns back to the colour charts. He gets bored really quickly, and looks around.*)

FRANKIE. God I hate it here.

MICHAEL. .

FRANKIE. Don't you hate it?

MICHAEL. *(Shrugs.)* It's alright.

FRANKIE. Oh my god as soon as I can, like, *as soon* as I can, I am getting Out Of Here!

MICHAEL. Maybe.

FRANKIE. I am!

MICHAEL. You'll be back.

FRANKIE. Won't.

MICHAEL. You will. Everyone does.

FRANKIE. Not me. Once I'm gone I'm gone.

(**MICHAEL** *snorts a laugh.*)

What?

MICHAEL. So dramatic!

FRANKIE. Nah it's shit! There's literally *nothing* to do!

MICHAEL. Yeah but, we find stuff to do.

FRANKIE. Getting stoned and setting fire to shit?

MICHAEL. *(To us.)* I can neither confirm nor deny.

FRANKIE. Hahaha!

MICHAEL. I dunno. It just, is what it is. It's better now I can drive.

FRANKIE. Oh my god, I can't wait to drive! Having to ask for a lift all the time is just, so dead. And the buses are shit. And the people are boring and it's just, so, depressing!

MICHAEL. Look, you go on and on that it's rubbish and there's nothin' here and blah blah, but you know, deep down, that this is the greatest place on earth/

FRANKIE. nah!

MICHAEL. It's home! It's your roots ain't it?! And you love it!

FRANKIE. Despite the delicate aroma of dead chickens and cider?

MICHAEL. Yeah! I like it!

FRANKIE. It's shit!

MICHAEL. Nah, it's pretty!

FRANKIE. Pretty?!

MICHAEL. Yeah. With like, trees and that? The fields and. I dunno, shuttup! I quite like it. And look, everyone's gotta be from somewhere. Why's it better to be from a big city than from round here?

FRANKIE. I'd way rather be from a big city! Oh my god! It's so cringe when someone asks *"oh where are you from"* and I'm like, yeah I'm from the back ass end of nowhere. And there's fuck all there, and it's shit. You're so lucky you can drive like!

MICHAEL. Yeah but. Still can't afford my own car. Dave's van is shit.

FRANKIE. It is a bit knackered mind.

MICHAEL. The engine is *battered!* Everytime I turn the key it sounds like an aeroplane taking off! Or a tractor!

FRANKIE. Oh my god you're becoming a Farmer Chav!

MICHAEL. Don't let 'em catch you calling 'em that!

FRANKIE. *(To us.)* Farmer Chavs are like, these gross lads who are always hanging around bus stops.

MICHAEL. Ain't it a bit offensive to call someone a chav?

FRANKIE. What? Yeah, well, I didn't *mean* it offensively.

MICHAEL. Yeah but it *is* definitely offensive, 'despite your intention'. Isn't that what you're always banging on at me/

FRANKIE. alright/

MICHAEL. oooh you got it wrong!

FRANKIE. Shuttup!

MICHAEL. *(Acknowledging us.)* Ah, you're embarrassed? It's OK! We all make mistakes/

FRANKIE. shuttup!

MICHAEL. Hey, hey Frankie, it's OK, we're *all* here for you, in this Teaching Moment!

FRANKIE. Wow I literally hate you!

MICHAEL. Hahaha gutted!

FRANKIE. *(To us.)* Anyway, these lads, formally known as Farmer Chavs though we will no longer refer to/

MICHAEL. You just did!

FRANKIE. Oh I give up!

MICHAEL. Ah! Don't sulk!

FRANKIE. I'm not!

MICHAEL. OK well while you're sulking I'll finish telling them. *(To us.)* These are local lads. Good enough but, a bit rough round the edges. Probably similar to city lads/

FRANKIE. *(To us.)* but on tractors!

MICHAEL. *(To us.)* Yeah. Drinking cheap cider and/

FRANKIE. *(To us.)* oh my god, the Wigmore lads *actually* drive their tractors to prom!

MICHAEL. They don't!

FRANKIE. They bloody do! I've seen it!

MICHAEL. That is jokes!

FRANKIE. *(To us.)* And they gender their tractors female, I mean what is that all about? Men naming their cars, or their boats/

MICHAEL. or their tractors/

FRANKIE. women's names?! They're like "oh yeah, I'm just gonna take Betty up the track"

MICHAEL. Ooh Betty! Hahaha!

FRANKIE. Why do men do that?

MICHAEL. It's the tracksuit with the gilet that gets me, and the/

BOTH. chelsea boots!

MICHAEL. Yeah! What a look!

FRANKIE. Ah but they're big softies underneath it all/

MICHAEL. yeah/

FRANKIE. you can tell. They've got hearts of gold like/

MICHAEL. oh yeah. Like with the garage fire?

FRANKIE. Oh my god yeah they were amazin'! Proper helping everyone out.

MICHAEL. Yeah they're actually sound like. Just maybe a bit attached to their tractors.

FRANKIE. Yeah... I can't wait 'til I can drive.

MICHAEL. I'll teach you.

FRANKIE. Will yer?!

MICHAEL. Corse. If mum says so.

FRANKIE. Oh god! Imagine the facebook post! *"Proud mum. My boys."*

MICHAEL. Is that what you want, to be a boy?

FRANKIE. .

MICHAEL. Is it?

FRANKIE. If you're just gonna take the piss/

MICHAEL. I'm not! I'm trying to understand. I'm genuinely trying to/

FRANKIE. *(Snapping.)* I've already explained it to you! *Months* ago! I sent you links of stuff to read. Loads of stuff that'd explain, podcasts and YouTube stuff and/

MICHAEL. *(To us.)* you wrapped your tiny hand, around my finger/

FRANKIE. I mean have you even looked at *any* of that?!

MICHAEL. *(To us.)* look! I'm your big brother.

FRANKIE. No?

MICHAEL. *(To us.)* You're my little sister.

FRANKIE. No, didn't think so.

> (**FRANKIE** *sulks.* **MICHAEL***'s phone rings. He looks at the caller ID and instantly tenses. He answers.)*

MICHAEL. Hello? ... Yeah, yeah I'm here now... Yeah it's almost done yeah... Yeah I know... I know... Yeah Dave, I know! ... Yeah, I'm *well* aware that they're a Big Client, I'm in their fucking house... Well I just... I'm sorry I just... Yeah... Yeah I *know!* ... Of *course* I ... Yeah. Right, yeah... Yeah, yeah Dave I'm on it! Trust me! ...

> (**MICHAEL** *looks at the phone. Dave has hung up.* **MICHAEL** *swears under his breath. A shudder of panic and rage flashes through* **MICHAEL***'s body.* **FRANKIE** *stares.* **MICHAEL** *swallows the movement back down. Stillness and silence.* **MICHAEL** *avoids* **FRANKIE***'s gaze.)*

FRANKIE. You alright?

MICHAEL. Yeah, course.

> *(Silence. They both paint.)*

FRANKIE. Why do you keep calling me your sister?

MICHAEL. .

FRANKIE. It's just so weird, cus like, you've actually always supported me, since forever. You've always treated me like I'm/

MICHAEL. *(Stern.)* I've got to get this done, today!

FRANKIE. I know!

> *(They paint. Until* **FRANKIE** *can't resist.)*

But it's just like, the words? Like you actually *see me*, in so many ways. But you won't use the right pronouns?

MICHAEL. I really fucking need to finish this/

FRANKIE. you just can't change the words? Can't make that shift in your/

MICHAEL. Frankie!

FRANKIE. *(To us.)* Like when I was getting bullied at school. For being fat. Which I actually wasn't, but like, the kids could see *something* was going on with me? Some kind of queerness? And obviously they didn't know the word for it, so they just called me fat. Which is, like, *so weird?!* Kids are weird! And *then,* oh my god, then, I had to be *Mary* in the nativity?! Fuck! And I cried *all* the way home about it. And mum was like, *"what's wrong with Mary? It's the main part! Who wouldn't want to be Mary?!"* Me! I didn't! Like oh my God this *horrible* white dress that was literally made from a table cloth!

MICHAEL. *(Laughing.)* And you'd cut your hair!

FRANKIE. Short like yours.

MICHAEL. *(Laughing.)* This proper dodgy kitchen-scissors job!

FRANKIE. I was seven!

MICHAEL. Exactly! And mum went, *mental!*

FRANKIE. Oh my God, her face!

MICHAEL. Marched you down the barbers to get it fixed. Which is actually, exactly you wanted in the first place?

FRANKIE. Yeah! Short back and sides please!

MICHAEL. You looked like a little lad.

FRANKIE. I *was* a little lad. That's the whole point.

MICHAEL. .

FRANKIE. Anyway, even with my new buzzcut they *still* cast me as Mary? Of all the girls they could have chosen in the class? I think they *knew*, and were doing it on purpose! Plonk me on stage in a table cloth dress.

MICHAEL. *(Laughing.)* That wig they found?!

FRANKIE. Ugh! Don't! I still have trauma about the wig!

MICHAEL. *(Laughing.)* Pigtails?!

FRANKIE. Don't, I'm triggered!

MICHAEL. *(Laughing.)* Like Britney Spears or summink?!

FRANKIE. So itchy! So stupid! Kept slipping off my head!

> (**MICHAEL** *laughs, doing an impression of* **FRANKIE** *trying to hold the wig on.*)

I told them I didn't want to do it. *Please* let me be Joseph! Or a shepherd? Or one of the three wise men? Please God let me be Jesus! The donkey? Anything but Mary! But they insisted!

> (**MICHAEL** *pulls out costumes from a paint pot. He quickly dresses them both in nativity gear.*)

So there I am. School hall. Centre stage. Table cloth dress and itchy Britney wig.

MICHAEL. *"A long time ago, a young woman named Mary."*

FRANKIE. Blushing my way through the lines.

MICHAEL. *"Lived in a village called Nazareth."*

FRANKIE. Trying not to cry.

MICHAEL. *"One day, an angel appeared to her."*

FRANKIE. And then, just when I didn't think it could get any worse. The plinky plonky piano starts.

> (**MICHAEL** *plays piano music off his phone.*)

MICHAEL. *(To us.)* Mr. Jefferson. Bless him. Took it very seriously.

FRANKIE. And I start proper panicking.

MICHAEL. *"Mary, you are blessed by God!"*

FRANKIE. Cus I know that any minute I'm going to have to sing.

MICHAEL. *"And will give birth to a son!"*

FRANKIE. A solo?!

MICHAEL. *"And name him Jesus!"*

FRANKIE. In front of everyone?!

MICHAEL. *"So Mary and Joseph started the long hard journey."*

FRANKIE. And like, singing is *really* not my favourite thing to do anyway, but especially when dressed like an angel on a Christmas tree! But like, the *shittest* Christmas tree you've ever seen, in like a security office of a shit warehouse or somethin'?!

MICHAEL. *"Mary and Joseph arrive in Bethlehem."*

FRANKIE. And I'm about to die! Or burst into flames, or like drown in my own tears/

MICHAEL. dramatic/

FRANKIE. and I look out. And I see you. And I see that you see, that this is hell for me. You *know*. You are the only one who really knows me, who really sees me properly.

MICHAEL. I'm sat next to mum, holding her hand as she tries not to cry. She's been crying a lot recently.

FRANKIE. What? No she wasn't.

MICHAEL. She was hiding it from you. But she lets me see. Late night crying on the sofa while you're asleep. Dad's

left, and she's sad all the time, and I'm the man of the
house now. I've got to take care of you.

FRANKIE. No/

MICHAEL. that's my job.

FRANKIE. No. He left *after* that. *After!* He/

MICHAEL. no.

FRANKIE. Yes! I remember! He was there!

MICHAEL. No/

FRANKIE. I remember/

MICHAEL. you've remembered it wrong.

FRANKIE. He was *there!* He saw the play, and he was
embarrassed, by me, because, because I was a shit
Mary, because I /...

MICHAEL. No/

FRANKIE. because I'm /... He was *embarrassed,* and so he/

MICHAEL. no. No! He left *ages* before that, months before!

FRANKIE. I/

MICHAEL. not because of *you!* Not *everything* is about
you!

FRANKIE. .

MICHAEL. .

FRANKIE. I see.

MICHAEL. I look up and I see you. And see that you have
no idea what's really going on. And that's the way it
should be, I mean, you're a kid.

FRANKIE. So were you!

MICHAEL. And this is the shittest Christmas ever. And I'm
trying to make it better, trying to look out for you/

FRANKIE. I look out, and see that you see/

MICHAEL. I have to be the one.

FRANKIE. That this is hell for me. You *know*.

MICHAEL. I am the only one/

FRANKIE. who really knows/

MICHAEL. it's *my* job to take care of you. So I get up.

FRANKIE. You just, *stand up?!* In the middle of Mr. Jefferson's piano interlude!

MICHAEL. I'm not even thinking, I just know I need to move.

FRANKIE. You stand up, in this sea of parents, sat staring at us.

MICHAEL. I just know you need my help.

FRANKIE. You run down the aisle of plastic seats and tinsel.

MICHAEL. I just know you need me.

FRANKIE. And you stand next to me.

MICHAEL. And hold your hand.

FRANKIE. And sing with me. Like the absolute hero you are.

> (*They sing Away in a Manger. They laugh.* **FRANKIE** *suddenly stops.*)

Oh my god, hang on, so that whole memory?! I thought you were really/

MICHAEL. I know! You were/

FRANKIE. I felt like, so seen/

MICHAEL. making it all about you/

FRANKIE. but fuck! It was actually all about you?!

MICHAEL. What?

FRANKIE. *(Laughing.)* You playing the hero? Deciding you've gotta swoop in and save the day and keep everyone safe?! Such a cis white man thing to do!

MICHAEL. I'm not!

FRANKIE. What?

MICHAEL. I'm not, *that!*

FRANKIE. What, cis?

MICHAEL. Yeah, I'm just a bloke!

FRANKIE. That's what that /...

> (**FRANKIE** *cracks up laughing.* **MICHAEL** *frowns.)*

MICHAEL. What's funny? Don't laugh at me!

FRANKIE. I'm not! I /... Look, let me explain it to you.

MICHAEL. nah, you're alright!

FRANKIE. Nah, hear me out! Right, it's like, these rules we tell ourselves, that are somehow about gender? And like, the boxes we put ourselves in? And how we think that means we have to behave. But, the boxes aren't real! So like, basically everyone's queer.

MICHAEL. What?!

FRANKIE. Yeah, cus like, gender is a social construct, so it doesn't really exist. So if you remove it then the boundaries don't/

MICHAEL. riiiiight?!

FRANKIE. No really! Just think about it!

MICHAEL. Nah, come on!

FRANKIE. What?

MICHAEL. You're just chatting shit!

FRANKIE. No/

MICHAEL. I'm not queer! Tasha ain't queer! Mum's not/

FRANKIE. she might be.

MICHAEL. Ugh! Don't!

FRANKIE. What? What's wrong with/

MICHAEL. just, don't!

FRANKIE. I'm just saying! I wish we didn't have these stupid rules, I wish everyone just let themselves be themselves.

MICHAEL. Right.

FRANKIE. It's like. *(To us.)* Oh God, how am I gonna explain this? *(Looking around the space for clues.)* OK. OK so, it's like *colours*, right?! So like, yeah! Yeah OK look, what if when you're born you're allowed all the colours. Every shade of every colour, all of them. Right you can paint with *any* colour you want, and it's great! It's really fun! It feels fucking great for everyone! Right, but then one day you suddenly given all these rules, like all of a sudden it's like *no, no you're not allowed Purple, oh no sorry you're not allowed Green, erm you're not supposed to have Orange!* Right these like unwritten rules that everyone somehow knows, and you feel a bit silly for not knowing so quickly you're like oh OK. And you put down Orange. And you *never* paint with it again. And you think you can't, when like, *you can!* Cus *everyone* can!

MICHAEL. What?

FRANKIE. Have Orange! You can have Orange!

MICHAEL. I don't like Orange.

FRANKIE. Well that's OK! You don't have to, the point, I'm trying to say, like, everyone should be allowed all the colours! It's *all* OK! And like, you might decide that you *don't* like Orange/

MICHAEL. I don't.

FRANKIE. Cool! That's really cool, if that's true for you/

MICHAEL. it is!

FRANKIE. Great, then no Orange for you, that's fine. But like, how sad is it that some people don't *allow* themselves Orange? Or Pink or Turquoise or whatever because of what they think other people will think about that? But like, what if *everyone* could paint with *all* the colours they wanted to, and not be judged for it, because it's cool, it's all cool, it's just *playing!* You're allowed to play! You have full permission to be playful with *all* the colours! You know?! Like, I just wish everyone knew that!

MICHAEL. Right!

FRANKIE. Why'd you do that?

MICHAEL. What?

FRANKIE. You always do that!

MICHAEL. What?

FRANKIE. Make me feel shit, after I've said something/

MICHAEL. I don't!

FRANKIE. You do! Everytime!

MICHAEL. Well maybe you shouldn't say such mad stuff?

FRANKIE. Yeah, yeah maybe.

MICHAEL. .

FRANKIE. Do you hate me?

MICHAEL. What? No, obviously not!

FRANKIE. Sometimes you act like you do/

MICHAEL. nah! I just /... Look, I just don't really/

FRANKIE. don't worry about it!

*(**FRANKIE** sulks. **MICHAEL** tries to catch their eye but they're not interested. They paint. **FRANKIE**'s phone pings. **FRANKIE** looks at it and instantly starts blushing. **MICHAEL** sees and laughs.)*

MICHAEL. Oh yeah?! Someone got you blushing!

FRANKIE. No!

MICHAEL. Yeah!

FRANKIE. No!

MICHAEL. *Yeah!*

FRANKIE. Little bit.

MICHAEL. You're *beetroot* mate! Oh my god proper beetroot!

FRANKIE. Shuttup!

MICHAEL. Can only mean one thing, naughty text! From a *boyyyy!* Or, a girl or/

FRANKIE. girl/

MICHAEL. right, cool, that's cool.

FRANKIE. It's my girlfriend.

MICHAEL. You've got a girlfriend!?!

FRANKIE. Yeah.

MICHAEL. Show us.

*(**FRANKIE** shows him his phone.)*

Woah! She's tidy!

FRANKIE. Yeah course! Don't sound so shocked!

MICHAEL. Nah but/

FRANKIE. I'm fit mate. Trust me, I got no problem getting a girl.

*(**MICHAEL** stares at **FRANKIE** like he's seeing him new. **FRANKIE** sees and pushes it further.)*

Trans people are hot.

*(**MICHAEL** squirms.)*

MICHAEL. Right.

FRANKIE. We are!

MICHAEL. OK!

FRANKIE. OK?

MICHAEL. Yeah, just /...

FRANKIE. What?

MICHAEL. Don't, just don't use that word, yeah?

FRANKIE. Trans?

MICHAEL. .

FRANKIE. Are you scared of the word?

MICHAEL. No! No, I'm not scared/

FRANKIE. trans! Trans trans trans! *(Dancing around.)* Trans trans trans! Trans trans trans trans/

MICHAEL. Frankie/

FRANKIE. trans trans trans I am trans! Fuck, that felt good! I am trans. My name is Frankie and I am trans/

MICHAEL. stop it!

FRANKIE. What?

MICHAEL. Just, stop it! Yeah? Fuck!

FRANKIE. What is your problem/

MICHAEL. you! You! Being all like *yay! Gay pride! Yay trans whatever!* Yay?! Like it's a good thing? Like it's OK?!

FRANKIE. It *is* OK/

MICHAEL. like you're not about to get beat up?! Like you're not about to get hated on by everyone? It's my job to take care of you!

FRANKIE. I don't need/

MICHAEL. you think you're being clever or like, cool or whatever?! But you're not, you're being fucking stupid! Just because you've got your new trendy college mates/

FRANKIE. what? That's not/

MICHAEL. and now it's like you're one of them ones. You sound like they do, saying all this stuff that you've *literally* never said before/

FRANKIE. I have!

MICHAEL. You've *never* spoken about *any* of this! Ever!

FRANKIE. I have! I've been questioning my gender since, forever/

MICHAEL. riiiight!

FRANKIE. Trying to, match? What I feel on the inside with, with what's happening and. And how people see me and/

MICHAEL. you're just a tomboy. And that's OK!

FRANKIE. Don't tell me what I am!

MICHAEL. Girls can like boys' stuff. Blue and football and, whatever! You're always banging on about that/

FRANKIE. that's not the same/

MICHAEL. girl power and all that?!

FRANKIE. It's not the same!

MICHAEL. I'm just saying, you've *changed!* Since going to college.

FRANKIE. So? So what if I have? *You've* changed since you met Tasha!

MICHAEL. I haven't!

FRANKIE. You have! Loads!

MICHAEL. Nah/

FRANKIE. and that's OK isn't it?! People change, that's normal?

MICHAEL. Yeah but/

FRANKIE. that's just growing up/

MICHAEL. yeah! But/

FRANKIE. what?

MICHAEL. I dunno, sometimes/

FRANKIE. what?!

MICHAEL. sometimes I can't keep up with you! Yeah like, oh right, here we go! *This* is the new thing is it? OK OK!

FRANKIE. This isn't a *phase* I'm going through! This is/

MICHAEL. what's it gonna be next? *Something*, for sure! And like *I'm* the dumb one for not *instantly* adjusting to whatever it is you've decided you are now? I'm stupid? I'm offensive for getting the words wrong, words what was *alright* yesterday but *today* they're not? So if I say *anything* then I'm being /... What's that word/

FRANKIE. transphobic/

MICHAEL. that! Now I'm suddenly *that?* Because I'm not *instantly* catching up with you, just overnight? I'm not magically OK with stuff that I ain't |OK with just cus *you* want me to be? Like suddenly *I'm stupid* and I'm this *terrible* person who's getting it all wrong *all* the time?! Like *I'm* wrong, because *you've* changed? When actually I'm just trying to get on with stuff?! Like, fuck, I'm getting *married! Tomorrow!* And you dump all this shit on me/

FRANKIE. no I'm not/

MICHAEL. the day before my wedding?!

FRANKIE. I've been trying to/

MICHAEL. I just want a *peaceful* life! I don't want all this drama *all* the time, I don't wanna talk about heavy shit *all* the time, and like, *how we're all fucking feeling* and, and, I dunno, how all the words I'm using are *wrong?!* And how I'm *so stupid* for not knowing when *I don't even wanna know!* I'm alright! But then you act like that makes me stupid, like I'm thick or/

FRANKIE. you're not thick/

MICHAEL. WELL I FUCKING FEEL IT!

FRANKIE. .

MICHAEL. .

FRANKIE. I /... I, I'm sorry that you/

MICHAEL. don't worry 'bout it!

FRANKIE. I didn't, I didn't mean to make you feel/

MICHAEL. just leave it!

> (**MICHAEL** *sulks. Bashing about with paint pots and brushes.* **FRANKIE** *pulls the collar of their T-shirt up to their chin, and speaks to us.*)

FRANKIE. Blue cocoon. Cotton ridge, pulled right up, sits snug on my eyebrows. Tucked my nose inside, to look, at skin. Painted turquoise from the light pouring through. My belly rises and falls in blue. It's hot in here, this cotton cave, the sound muffled somehow as I look, at my body. Fascinated. Like woah, I live inside of there? *That's* my body? That's the edge of me, where I stop and the rest of the world begins. I giggle at skin. Seems so silly somehow.

> (**FRANKIE** *pulls the T-shirt up over their eyebrows.* **MICHAEL** *looks at* **FRANKIE** *and sees he's got a moment to be alone with us. Movement starts sneaking out of his body despite his best attempts to calm himself.*)

MICHAEL. I'm trying, I'm *really* trying but I /... I /... I'm working so hard to be the man I want to be but, fuck! Sometimes I just /... I get so stressed out by it all, like how'd you *do* all of that? How do people *do* all of it? /... Juggle all of it and /... Be everything to everyone and /... I just need to get this done I need to get this done I need to /... Keep Dave happy, keep my mum, keep Frankie /... Give Tasha the Dream Wedding! I just need to /... Cus fuck, when you really think about it? Life is huge! Really really, huge! And I'm /... I'm /... Tiny. And I dunno how we all do it?

> (**FRANKIE** *pulls their T-shirt back down to speak to us.*)

FRANKIE. It's late summer. Gorgeous and warm. Everyone's all sticky in shorts, complaining about the heat. But it's nice. The smell of BBQs and suncream fills the air. Long days are stretched out, so we're out late, kicking a ball about on the field by our estate. The grass is all sun bleached and golden.

MICHAEL. Poetic.

FRANKIE. It was!

MICHAEL. More burnt to be honest. Burnt in the sun. Dry, yellow/

FRANKIE. sun bleached and *beautiful!* Dusty earth kicked up by cheap trainers/

MICHAEL. fake brands or nicked.

FRANKIE. Sold off the back of a lorry in Hightown.

MICHAEL. Adidas with the four stripes!

FRANKIE. Scuffed the toe caps already!

MICHAEL. Oi! Mum will go mad!

FRANKIE. Don't care today!

MICHAEL. Cus today's Sunday!

FRANKIE. Sun dazed Sunday!

MICHAEL. Sun scorched patch of grass in the middle of our estate is our football pitch. Our stadium! Our empire!

FRANKIE. The team is three local lads, Michael and me.

MICHAEL. It's all *very* serious.

FRANKIE. A terrible tackle has sent you crashing to the ground.

MICHAEL. Oh shit!

FRANKIE. Cut my knee, and my palm look!

MICHAEL. You alright?!

FRANKIE. Yeah I'll be fine!

MICHAEL. Good!

FRANKIE. Blood pours down my shin and onto my socks/

MICHAEL. but you were brave!

FRANKIE. So brave!

MICHAEL. You get a penalty!

FRANKIE. Oh God, OK!

You step up to the ball.

Blink sweat out of sunny eyes.

MICHAEL. You take your time/

FRANKIE. sweat making my skin sting/

MICHAEL. prepare well, like I taught you.

FRANKIE & MICHAEL. Take a deep breath/

MICHAEL. and/

FRANKIE. and/

MICHAEL. you boot it! And/

FRANKIE. and/

MICHAEL. and it goes straight in!

FRANKIE & MICHAEL. YES!

FRANKIE. Top bins!

MICHAEL. And we're all going mental/

FRANKIE. like this is Wembley/

MICHAEL. and you just won the World Cup!

FRANKIE. Zoom around cheering/

MICHAEL. whip our tops off and swing 'em round our 'eads!

FRANKIE. I see you all take your shirt off and I want that!

MICHAEL. Yes Frankie yes!

FRANKIE. I want that freedom/

MICHAEL. Yes Frankie!

FRANKIE. Want that air on my skin/

MICHAEL. Frankiiiiiiie!

FRANKIE. Want to feel like you look/

MICHAEL. yesssss!

FRANKIE. So I pull mine off too and /... I've not got a bra on or nothing. I'm like, twelve, maybe thirteen. So it's

like, sort of still OK? Maybe? I dunno I think I forgot,
I was so in the game and in the heat of the day and
I forgot my body's not, mine. So I took off my top and/

MICHAEL. and yeah, one of the lads laughs/

FRANKIE. they *all* laugh.

MICHAEL. But, but they're just messing about!

FRANKIE. They *all* laugh at me/

MICHAEL. yeah but not like, not like *serious,* it's not like/

FRANKIE. you laugh too.

MICHAEL. .

FRANKIE. I watch you. Laughing at me/

MICHAEL. well it was fucking funny! What can I say?!

FRANKIE. Shove my shirt back on. Prickly eyes and
burning hot, want to rip my own skin off!

MICHAEL. Come on lads!

FRANKIE. Want to *rip* my own skin off!

MICHAEL. I get the ball/

FRANKIE. want to rip my own/

MICHAEL. take it up the pitch/

FRANKIE. want to rip/

MICHAEL. *(Snapping.)* OK! OK we get it!

FRANKIE. No, I don't think you do. In fact I think that
is *exactly* the problem. You don't get it, and you don't
wanna make *any* effort to. Cus it's *uncomfortable* for
you. And you get to opt out of uncomfortable. Cus
you're a bloke. A straight cis white/

MICHAEL. oh come on/

FRANKIE. that's the truth though innit?! You don't have to look at stuff/

MICHAEL. oh don't get all/

FRANKIE. what/

MICHAEL. political and/

FRANKIE. *it is fucking political!*

MICHAEL. *(Silly voice.)* OK OK! Whatever you say!

> (**MICHAEL** *laughs.* **FRANKIE** *doesn't.*
> **MICHAEL** *pulls a face to us.*)

Ooh! I've upset her.

FRANKIE. Them. Or Him.

MICHAEL. What?

FRANKIE. I'm nonbinary. I'm queer. I'm trans. My pronouns are/

MICHAEL. right!

FRANKIE. You can't ignore it forever/

MICHAEL. can't I?!

FRANKIE. You actually hurting me, by refusing/

MICHAEL. oh I'm hurting you? Oh I am sorry, so terribly sorry.

FRANKIE. Are you incapable of talking honestly? About real stuff?

MICHAEL. Guess so. Can you pass the roller?

FRANKIE. .

MICHAEL. No? Get it myself then.

FRANKIE. D'you know I've always looked up to you. You've literally been my hero, forever. Wanting to be like you. To be liked, by you, wanting your approval, all the time. Wanting you to think that I'm alright. But fuck it! Honestly! Fuck it! You're not my hero anymore! Oh my God, I can't believe I wasted so much time chasing you, desperate for you to understand me. When you ain't never gonna bother to understand anyone but yourself. Never gonna even *try* to think about what someone else might be going through?! Nah! Cus you just bumble your way through your days, through your easy little life, where you've got everything handed to you on a plate.

MICHAEL. What have I got?

FRANKIE. Oh my God you don't even know! You are the pinnacle of privilege!

MICHAEL. What?

FRANKIE. You are so privileged it's mad!

MICHAEL. Privileged? I can't even fucking spell it!

FRANKIE. That's not th/

MICHAEL. if I'm so privileged then how comes I'm busting a gut to pay rent and help mum out, to cover her bills, to buy *your* fucking trainers? *I'm* privileged?! Hah! Where?

FRANKIE. That's about class, that's not/

MICHAEL. what? Not part of this privilege thing? Think it might be. Think it fucking should be. Cus it feels shit mate! I'm at the top of nothin'!

FRANKIE. You have got life so easy!

MICHAEL. What?

FRANKIE. Never have to think fuck, what if I really have to chose, between being who I am and being loved by my family?!

MICHAEL. That's not what/

FRANKIE. you never have to worry about that, do you? Ever! *"Oh I just wanna have a peaceful life!"* Fuck Michael! How fucking privileged is that?

MICHAEL. Listen, that's not what I/

FRANKIE. you get to be OK, *all* the time. Never anything wrong with you, you're just OK, all the time?!

MICHAEL. No, no that's not/

FRANKIE. how you doing Michael? *"Yeah I'm sound mate! I'm good! I'm OK yeah!"* Always OK, all the time, no complaints!

MICHAEL. No, no that's not true I /... I/

FRANKIE. what?

MICHAEL. I /...

FRANKIE. What?

MICHAEL. I /...

FRANKIE. Nothing. See! You've got *nothing* to say, because actually you're just/

> (**MICHAEL** *explodes into dance. It's fast and furious. He's searching for something in his body.* **FRANKIE** *stares, in awe and alarmed. It builds and builds and builds and eventually* **FRANKIE** *is scared by it, and when he can't take it anymore he physically stops* **MICHAEL**. **MICHAEL** *stands still, staring straight ahead. Sweat and emotion pouring out of his body.* **MICHAEL** *catches his breath. It takes as long as it takes.* **FRANKIE** *is really moved by it, but unable to move.)*

MICHAEL. I'm not OK.

FRANKIE. What?

MICHAEL. I'm not OK. You think I am, but I'm actually /...

FRANKIE. .

MICHAEL. .

FRANKIE. Fuck.

MICHAEL. .

FRANKIE. Why didn't you tell me?

MICHAEL. .

FRANKIE. Why didn't you, I dunno /... Fuck.

MICHAEL. I went to doctors.

FRANKIE. No.

MICHAEL. Got bad like, needed to do something.

FRANKIE. No.

MICHAEL. Got medication.

FRANKIE. No.

MICHAEL. Why do you keep saying no?

FRANKIE. You're fine! You're *fine!* You don't, you don't
need that, you're, you're just /... I maybe I could, I/

MICHAEL. what? What could you do, what could anyone
do? When I'm like that no one can help me, seriously
it's like, like there's no point/

FRANKIE. stop it/

MICHAEL. can't see the point, in *anything*/

FRANKIE. no/

MICHAEL. and Tasha, she has been *so good* to me! So
patient and kind and /... Fuck! I don't deserve her, I
really don't she, she don't deserve all this *shit* it's too
much to deal with/

FRANKIE. no/

MICHAEL. *I'm* too much to/

FRANKIE. no/

MICHAEL. why would anyone want to put up with me eh?!
Why would anyone wanna love me?

FRANKIE. Stop it! Stop! Stop talking like that! You're fine!
You're *fine!*

MICHAEL. No/

FRANKIE. you are! You are you just need/

MICHAEL. you're not listening! I'm trying to explain, and
you're/

FRANKIE. I don't want to hear it! Ok?! I don't wanna
fucking hear it!

MICHAEL. .

FRANKIE. .

MICHAEL. .

FRANKIE. Fuck!

MICHAEL. Yeah.

FRANKIE. Oh my God, I've been so selfish?! I've, I've just
been, thinking about me? I haven't even *noticed* that
you/

MICHAEL. yeah. Well. You've had a lot going on.

FRANKIE. Yeah but, so have you! I would never have got
you to do this, if I'd know that you/

MICHAEL. nah I wanted to! It's important. There's all that
mad shit in the papers, and online and that, all the time.
People writing about people like you? When really they
don't know nothin'! I mean that was the whole point,
wasn't it? Of us being here? Doing our story?

FRANKIE. Yeah.

MICHAEL. Cus you said we get stuck, sometimes, all of us.
We get stuck in the stories we tell ourselves?

FRANKIE. And each other yeah. And we don't *really* listen, and it's all really binary. Really like, *I'm right you're wrong*/

MICHAEL. black and white?

FRANKIE. Yeah *this or that*. But like, we're all *way* more complicated than that!

MICHAEL. Yeah.

FRANKIE. Yeah so I wanted people to hear *our* story. Cus like, *you* didn't get it for ages.

MICHAEL. Nah/

FRANKIE. and it was horrible, but now you do.

MICHAEL. Starting to, yeah.

FRANKIE. So maybe someone else might. Maybe someone might see me and not think about the stuff they've read, but like actually remember that I actually am a human. And like, not be so freaked out by it all.

MICHAEL. Thanks.

FRANKIE. For what?

MICHAEL. All of it. Being you. Forcing me to do this/

FRANKIE. I didn't *force* you/

MICHAEL. doing our story. Cus yeah, I reckon it's good for me too. Even if it hurts like.

FRANKIE. Yeah.

MICHAEL. Yeah. So, what happens next?

FRANKIE. I dunno.

MICHAEL. What?

FRANKIE. I dunno! But we can't just be *stuck?* Like *this?!* Angry, and hurting and/

MICHAEL. no! Be the shittest ending ever! But I mean, I dunno, how to/

FRANKIE. me neither.

MICHAEL. I dunno, what to/

FRANKIE. me neither.

MICHAEL. Guess we're double fucked then!

FRANKIE. Guess so!

> (**MICHAEL** *suddenly walks to his starting position of the play.* **FRANKIE** *watches, confused.*)

MICHAEL. You walk in. And...

FRANKIE. What are you doing?

MICHAEL. We look at each other, and...

FRANKIE. Why are you going back?

MICHAEL. Because we did your version, and now this is my one.

FRANKIE. *My* version? My version is the truth!

MICHAEL. Well I'm rewriting it.

FRANKIE. You can't!

MICHAEL. We can.

FRANKIE. .

MICHAEL. You walk in, and/

FRANKIE. .

MICHAEL. we know. We both know/

FRANKIE. that *this* is a Big moment.

MICHAEL. Huge! It feels/

FRANKIE. huge/

MICHAEL. and we're suddenly really awake, to everything. We're standing, toe to toe/

FRANKIE. nose to nose/

MICHAEL. soul to soul. And I dunno where to start?

FRANKIE. I dunno/

MICHAEL. so we both start/

FRANKIE & MICHAEL. speaking at the same time.

MICHAEL. You're like/

FRANKIE. I need to talk to you. But you're like/

MICHAEL. *(To him.)* no! I'm sorry, but I can't do this right now.

FRANKIE. But that's not what you said! You were *way* harsher than that!

MICHAEL. I'm sorry, but I've got a lot going on, and I/

FRANKIE. you never wanna talk/

MICHAEL. please/

FRANKIE. you never wanna listen! You're so selfish/

MICHAEL. *I'm* selfish?! Wow!

FRANKIE. So selfish! You've got everything! You've literally got it made but you can't. Hang on, we're just fighting again!

MICHAEL. I know! Fuck! Well, I dunno how to/

FRANKIE. OK, OK, OK what if I just don't say anything. And you just talk. Go on!

MICHAEL. Right, erm. Well. I, I think that/

FRANKIE. you think that I should wear the dress to 'keep the peace'/

MICHAEL. Frankie/

FRANKIE. but you're failing to understand how *awful* that's going to be for me and/

MICHAEL. Frankie!

FRANKIE. Yeah I know I know, I'm sorry I can't help it! Fuck! This is hard!

MICHAEL. We're running out of time.

FRANKIE. I know!

MICHAEL. I can't, *cancel* the wedding, cus we're fighting/

FRANKIE. I know!

MICHAEL. And we can't stay *here*, stuck in this bit of the story!

FRANKIE. I know!

MICHAEL. So how are we gonna get to the happy ending?

FRANKIE. Well, maybe that's the problem.

MICHAEL. What?

FRANKIE. Maybe we're trapped in some hetero-ghetto story-telling shape, and we need to do something different, something queer!

MICHAEL. Erm, like what?

FRANKIE. Like, *our* version of the ending. Something that's *true* to us. Cus like, OK we're at that bit they call The Low Point.

MICHAEL. In stories like?

FRANKIE. Yeah, this is where the characters look proper doomed. The Good Guy has been caught by the Bad Guy/

MICHAEL. and he's about to be killed?

FRANKIE. Yeah, in some really horrible way/

MICHAEL. and then the whole world is about to be blown up! And you're watching like oh my God how the fuck are they gonna get out of that?!

FRANKIE. Yeah. But like, for us it's maybe a bit less dramatic.

MICHAEL. But still, this is like, yeah, proper heavy gear innit. Like OK, I know neither of us wanted to go off the deep end but, I dunno. Life *is* heavy sometimes ain't it?

FRANKIE. Yeah, it is... You know what we've gotta do, right?

MICHAEL. Ignore all this like it never happened, and just, go to the pub?

FRANKIE. Haha no! We've got to face it, head on!

MICHAEL. Right.

FRANKIE. Really *talk* about stuff!

MICHAEL. Right.

FRANKIE. Be *honest* with how we're feeling!

MICHAEL. Right. Well that sounds really fuckin' hard like.

FRANKIE. Yeah.

MICHAEL. And, a bit American?

FRANKIE. Yeah, but you know it's right. This is the hard bit, the bit where we're brave. The bit in the story that's usually the Big Battle Scene.

MICHAEL. Do I get a sword?

FRANKIE. Yeah, if you like.

MICHAEL. 'mazin'!

> (*They prepare for the big battle scene. Pulling battle armour out of paint pots. It's very serious. Music. Lights. They dance on the*

spot, pulsing with energy, building and building. They face each other with paint brushes in their hands. They speak to us.)

This is the Big Battle Scene!

FRANKIE. Where usually the Good Guy would fight the Bad Guy.

MICHAEL. The Hero would fight the Monster.

FRANKIE. Or slay the dragon.

MICHAEL. Or kill the beast.

FRANKIE. But in this story there is no beast.

MICHAEL. Except for like, the one in our heads?

FRANKIE. Yeah.

MICHAEL. Like a metaphor?

FRANKIE. Yeah! A metaphorical beast! This is where we battle our metaphorical beast and face our deepest fears.

MICHAEL. Right. And we do it together, yeah?

FRANKIE. Yeah!

MICHAEL. Good!

FRANKIE. Let's do this!

> *(They let out a battle cry and make their way through a metaphorical jungle to find the metaphorical beast. They swipe at imaginary monsters, and get points when they kill one. It's fast paced and energetic, taking over the whole space.)*

OK here we go! So, you get points for being honest, and points for being brave!

MICHAEL. Right. OK, you go first!

FRANKIE. OK. Are you actually depressed or are you just like, moaning?

MICHAEL. Fuck! Ouch Frankie!

FRANKIE. I'm sorry!

MICHAEL. Is that your first one?

FRANKIE. Yeah. And I get a point, *ping!* Cus it were brave.

MICHAEL. OK. Wow OK, right. Erm, no! No, I actually am depressed. Doctors said so. I'm on meds and that. It's official.

FRANKIE. OK.

MICHAEL. Why is that so hard for you to get?

FRANKIE. I dunno!

MICHAEL. *(Buzzer sound.)* Eh-err!

FRANKIE. Fuck! Erm, OK, cus it's scary?

MICHAEL. *Ping!* Yeah!

FRANKIE. I'm scared.

MICHAEL. *Ping!* Great!

FRANKIE. I'm scared of you being sad, of you being ill.

MICHAEL. *Ping!*

FRANKIE. Cus I want you to be my big brother who's always there and always OK and always gonna protect me like. Fuck. Yeah I think that's true. *Ping!*

MICHAEL. Well done!

FRANKIE. Thanks. OK, you go!

MICHAEL. Right OK. Erm. You sure?

FRANKIE. Yeah! Hit me with it.

MICHAEL. OK. Are you actually, like, trans, or are you just jumping on some bandwagon like?

FRANKIE. Bandwagon?

MICHAEL. Yeah cus, like it's in the papers a lot ain't it? And it's all a bit/

FRANKIE. what?

MICHAEL. Trendy or whatever/

FRANKIE. trendy?!

MICHAEL. Yeah! Are you like, just tryna be cool?

FRANKIE. Wow?!

MICHAEL. *Ping!* I get a ping?

FRANKIE. Yeah OK yeah, ping for you. And no! I'm not trying to be cool. I actually am trans, I mean, I think I'm nonbinary, trans masc? I dunno. The categories do my head in. I'm still trying to work it all out. *Ping!*

MICHAEL. I just dunno why you'd choose this? *Ping!*

FRANKIE. You think it's a choice? *(Laughing.)* A lifestyle choice?!

MICHAEL. I, I dunno I! It just seems so hard!

FRANKIE. Yeah it is!

MICHAEL. I just, I don't want your life to be harder than it/

FRANKIE. trying to be a girl, when you're not, is really hard! It's impossible! *Ping!* It's making me not want to be here anymore. *Ping!* And you're making it harder. *Ping!*

MICHAEL. I'm just trying to protect you! *Ping!*

FRANKIE. You can't, not from everyone! *Ping!*

MICHAEL. I'm your big brother! It's my job to keep you safe.

FRANKIE. No, it's my job to keep me safe.

MICHAEL. I don't want people to hurt you, to think you're, like, /...

FRANKIE. What?

MICHAEL. I dunno!

FRANKIE. Like what?!

MICHAEL. Like, a weirdo? *Ping!*

FRANKIE. I *am* a weirdo! *Ping!*

MICHAEL. No seriously. I don't want people/

FRANKIE. you don't want people to think *you're* a weirdo. *Ping!* So you're trying to stop me/

MICHAEL. no! That's not it!

FRANKIE. It is! *Ping ping ping!*

MICHAEL. I don't wanna lose you! *Ping!*

FRANKIE. What?

MICHAEL. I don't want you to change! *Ping!* You're my sister!

FRANKIE. Brother! Fucksake! Are you ever gonna get that?! *Fuck!* No, this isn't working! I was stupid for thinking this was ever gonna work. You're never gonna/

MICHAEL. I love you.

FRANKIE. *(Stopping dead.)* Fuck! You never say that!

MICHAEL. Well, I do. *Ping!*

FRANKIE. I love you n all.

BOTH. *Ping!*

FRANKIE. Which is why I need you to/

MICHAEL. I know. I'm trying. I want you to be happy.

FRANKIE. I am, I'm *much* happier like this. Cus I was *always* this, underneath it all, like/

MICHAEL. like, a wrapping?

FRANKIE. Yeah! Like a wrapping yeah, on a/

MICHAEL. easter egg? Is that a bit stupid?

FRANKIE. No! It's brilliant! It's like, that's it exactly! It's like, the egg, the chocolate, it's still the same. No matter what box it's in/

MICHAEL. right/

FRANKIE. if you took it out, and put it in another box, it'd taste the same/

MICHAEL. yeah/

FRANKIE. cus that's just the bloody wrapping/

MICHAEL. yeah/

FRANKIE. and no one cares about the wrapping! We just care about the chocolate!

MICHAEL. Well, yeah/

FRANKIE. and how it tastes/

MICHAEL. yeah. And how big it is.

FRANKIE. Well, yeah, I mean that's like, a bit problematic, for this metaphor but/

MICHAEL. so is that what you're doing? Changing your box?

FRANKIE. Yeah. Cus the last one I was in was killing me. *Ping!* And like, more than that. What I'm saying is, what I'm *learning* is like, *why/*

MICHAEL. why do we put chocolate in boxes at all?!

FRANKIE. Yes!

BOTH. *Ping!*

MICHAEL. Yeah. Like, why do we assume right, that some chocolate should be in a certain box, and some in another/

FRANKIE. yes!

MICHAEL. When like, we never fucking ask the chocolate itself, what box would you like to be in mate?

FRANKIE. Yes! Exactly! *Ping! Ping! Ping!*

MICHAEL. I get it. Yeah, that's mad! Cus like, *I* got put in a box right, and like, no fucker asked me. I just got shoved into a box, soon as I was born like. They looked at my body, looked at my bits and went, *right, into that box there then lad!* And it's just by chance really, that actually, *I* quite like the box I've been put in. I think it's alright like, I'm quite happy in my box but, but that's just like, dead lucky ain't it?!

FRANKIE. Dead fuckin' lucky! Cus like if you *hate* the box you've been put in/

MICHAEL. and it don't fit right, and you have to like/

FRANKIE. bend right out of shape/

MICHAEL. to try to fit, and try to like/

FRANKIE. *breathe*?! Yeah.

MICHAEL. And like, it's all you've ever known?! So you don't even *think* to question the box you're in/

FRANKIE. you just start to question *yourself*, and blame *yourself*.

MICHAEL. Fuck!

FRANKIE. Like oh maybe if I was *better* then/

MICHAEL. I'd fit better in this box?

FRANKIE. Yeah.

MICHAEL. And so you try and you try and you try and you try to fit, over and over, but you don't *ever* fit right. And you feel completely fucking mental for not fitting! And like, you *hate* yourself and *blame* yourself and it's *fucking horrible!* But like it were never your fault!

It were the box's fault all along should never have been
in that fucking box in the first place should never have
been in any fucking box at all!

FRANKIE. .

MICHAEL. Sorta like that?

FRANKIE. You're brilliant. I fucking love you.

MICHAEL. Soppy sod. True though innit?

FRANKIE. Yeah! And like, same for you. You don't have to
be ok, if you're not. You don't have to pretend/

MICHAEL. yeah/

FRANKIE. cus you think that's like manly or whatever.

MICHAEL. That's a box too.

FRANKIE. Yeah!

MICHAEL. Yeah. It's like, stop putting people in boxes!

> *(Music swells as they do one big final slay of
> the metaphorical beast, slashing their way
> across the space with imaginary swords. Like
> classic heroes in a huge Hollywood movie.
> They speak in the movie-trailer-man voice.)*

No more playing the hero!

FRANKIE. No more chasing approval!

MICHAEL. No more boxes!

FRANKIE. No more fucking boxes!

MICHAEL. No more shit haircuts!

> *(Music cuts.)*

(Laughing.) Sorry I couldn't help myself!

FRANKIE. Well d'you know what, I like my hair, even if you
don't.

MICHAEL. Good for you.

FRANKIE. Shuttup!

>(**MICHAEL**'s *phone rings.*)

MICHAEL. Bloody 'ell... Oh it's Dave... Dave? Yeah... Yeah we're almost done... My brother came to help out... My brother. Frankie... Yeah... Yeah well, we got it wrong... Yeah... Cool, cool. Yeah. Yeah OK, catch you later. Alright.

>(**FRANKIE** *is beaming. They burst into dance, joyful and vibrant. They speak to us as they dance.*)

FRANKIE. You walk in! And/

MICHAEL. we look at each other!

FRANKIE. And we know!

BOTH. We both know!

MICHAEL. That this is a Big moment!

BOTH. Huge!

>(*They pull out wedding suits from the paint pots and put them on.*)

FRANKIE. We're standing/

MICHAEL. toe to toe/

FRANKIE. nose to nose/

MICHAEL. soul to soul.

FRANKIE. And I look into your eyes. And you look into mine.

MICHAEL. And I see you seeing/

BOTH. me.

MICHAEL. And something inside of me is telling me/

FRANKIE. to pay attention/

MICHAEL. to watch this moment we're in/

FRANKIE. because we know/

MICHAEL. That *this* right here, could be the start/

FRANKIE. or the end, of something.

MICHAEL. Of everything! And I dunno where to start?

FRANKIE. I dunno/

BOTH. so we both/

MICHAEL. start speaking/

BOTH. at the same time.

FRANKIE. You're like/

MICHAEL. I need to talk to you. But you're like/

FRANKIE. so do I.

MICHAEL. And we realise that/

FRANKIE. we're not very good at this!

MICHAEL. No!

FRANKIE. No!

MICHAEL. But we're going to try.

FRANKIE. Yeah. We're really gonna try.

Ingram Content Group UK Ltd.
Milton Keynes UK
UKHW020629160323
418667UK00016B/1479

9 780573 013584